Essential

SERIES

COMPREHENSIVE, STEP-BY-STEP COOKING

Asian Dishes

HINKLER
BOOKS

HINKLER BOOKS

Essential Cooking Series: Asian Dishes
First published in 2009 by Hinkler Books Pty Ltd
45–55 Fairchild Street
Heatherton Victoria 3202 Australia
www.hinklerbooks.com

Disclaimer: The nutritional information listed under each recipe does not
include the nutrient content of garnishes or any accompaniments not listed
in specific quantitites in the ingredient list. The nutritional information for
each recipe is an estimate only, and may vary depending on the brand of
ingredients used, and due to natural biological variations in the composition
of natural foods such as meat, fish, fruit and vegetables. The nutritional
information was calculated by using Foodworks dietary analysis software
(Version 3, Xyris Software Pty Ltd, Highgate Hill, Queensland, Australia) based
on the Australian food composition tables and food manufacturers' data.
Where not specified, ingredients are always analysed as average or medium,
not small or large.

ISBN: 978 1 7418 5715 3

10 9 8 7 6 5 4 3 2
14 13 12 11 10

Printed and bound in China

Contents

introduction   4–9

starters   10–17

poultry and meat   18–29

seafood   30–37

vegetarian   38–39

desserts   40–41

glossary   42–43

conversions   44–45

index   46

An introduction to Asian dishes

The largest continent on earth, Asia is home to an exciting and diverse range of cuisines. In Western countries, Chinese, Japanese, Indian, Thai and Vietnamese food outlets have been a welcome addition to the restaurant scene. The popularity of Asian food has grown immeasurably and with it a desire to make this cuisine part of home-cooked family meals. Supermarkets now stock a considerable range of the necessary Asian ingredients – grocery lines and fresh Asian vegetables, herbs and flavourings. This book will help you to prepare a wonderful Asian meal, packed full of flavour.

STOCKING THE PANTRY

The following guide will assist you to select a basic supply.

SAUCES

Listed are the most widely used Asian sauces – it is essential to stock 2–3 of these in your pantry.

SOY SAUCE: A thin brown sauce made from soy beans, wheat, yeast and salt. It is aged and distilled to make the sauce. It is widely used in Asian cooking. Light soy sauce is light in colour and density and will flavour foods without adding colour. Dark soy sauce is darker, thicker and richer in flavour as it is aged longer than the light soy. It gives a rich brown colour to the food. Indonesian soy, or kecap manis, is thick, dark and sweet. For a similar result use dark soy sauce and add brown sugar. All soy sauces will keep indefinitely on the pantry shelf.

OYSTER SAUCE: This sauce is made by fermenting dried oysters with soy sauce and brine. It adds a rich savoury flavour to meat and vegetable dishes and is also used in stir-fries. Be sure to store it in the refrigerator after opening.

HOISIN SAUCE: Hoisin is made from fermented soy beans, garlic, chilli and spices. Sweet and spicy in flavour, it is used as a condiment or to add to pork, chicken or beef dishes. It can be interchanged with oyster sauce in recipes, and can be stored on a pantry shelf.

CHILLI SAUCE: Various varieties are available. Choose one to suit your tastes. Chinese sweet chilli sauce is a hot sweet-and-sour sauce. It is added in small quantities to fish dishes and stir-fries. Thai chilli sauce, or náam phrík, is used mainly as a table condiment. Some are hot and strong, flavoured with shrimp paste and fish sauce. Milder varieties are available and are used as a dipping sauce.

Store these sauces in the refrigerator after opening.

FISH SAUCE: An important ingredient in South-East Asian cuisine. A little added to the cooking has a major impact on flavour. It is made from fermented whitebait and salt. Fish sauce adds a pungent flavour to dipping sauces, soups, stir-fries, rice, noodles and salad dressings. It can be stored on a pantry shelf.

BLACK BEAN SAUCE: Made from fermented black soy beans, chilli and spices. Used in meat stir-fries, or mixed stir-fries. Hot bean or sweet bean sauce is available. It should be stored in the refrigerator after opening.

SHRIMP SAUCE: Much like fish sauce but made with small shrimps or prawns and brine. It resembles anchovy paste, which is often used as a substitute. It can be stored on the pantry shelf.

SPICES, CURRY AND OTHER FLAVOURING AGENTS

FIVE-SPICE POWDER: A very popular spice in Chinese cookery. It is a ground mixture of anise, pepper, star anise, cloves, cinnamon and fennel.

TURMERIC: A plant root that has been dried and powdered. It gives a mild flavour, but is prized for the colour it gives to food, particularly rice. It is included in curry powder mixes for that purpose.

CUMIN: An essential ingredient in prepared curry powder mixes. It has a delightful fragrance and goes well with beef and lamb.

DRIED CORIANDER SEED OR GROUND CORIANDER (CILANTRO): The dried seeds of the fresh coriander (cilantro) plant. It gives a delightful fragrance to food.

TAMARIND LIQUID: Tamarind liquid is an important flavouring agent in Indian, Indonesian and Malayan cooking. The long fibres of the tamarind pod are soaked in water to extract the flavour, the pulp is discarded and the liquid is used. Dried tamarind pulp is sold in packets. There is also a bottled tamarind liquid available, perhaps not as good as soaking the pulp to make the liquid.

CURRY: Curry is the word that refers to the sauce around braised meat and chicken. The spice mixes used to make curry in India and South-East Asia are individually blended according to the fragrance and strength of heat desired. For convenience, curry powder (a ready-mixed blend of spices for the sauce) became commercially available a long time ago. The blends now cater to a wider range of tastes. Curry pastes, which are spice blends roasted in oil, come in particular spice blends; eg Thai red or green curry paste and rendang curry paste. In your pantry, stock a mild and fragrant curry powder or paste. If a hotter taste is required, add a little chilli powder. Store dry powders on the pantry shelf and curry pastes in the refrigerator after opening.

DRIED SHRIMPS: A little dried shrimp is used to give a delightful flavour to food. Soak as directed and store in a tightly closed jar on a pantry shelf.

WHITE MISO: Important in Japanese cuisine, it's used to flavour stocks and soups. It is made from yellow soy beans, boiled and crushed, then allowed to ferment. It should be stored in the refrigerator.

RICE WINE: A wine made from rice. Mirin, a sweet rice wine, is also used.

DRY AND SWEET SHERRY: If you are fond of Chinese cooking, a bottle of either is useful in your pantry.

RICE VINEGAR: Rice vinegar is clear to pale gold in colour, with a mildly sweet flavour. It's used in dipping sauces and salad dressings. A little sweet sherry may be substituted.

PALM SUGAR: Palm sugar is obtained from the sap of the coconut and palmyra palm trees. It has a strong, sweet flavour. Dark brown sugar is a good substitute.

RICE AND DRIED NOODLES

Rice and dried noodles are the staples of Asian cuisine and you should always have a cache readily available in your pantry.

SHORT-GRAIN OR MEDIUM-GRAIN RICE: These varieties are used mainly in Chinese cooking.

JASMINE AND BASMATI: Both are a long-grain rice and are preferred for Indian and Malaysian dishes.

GLUTINOUS RICE: Also known as sticky rice, this rice is used mainly in sweet dishes. It clings together when cooked and blends well with sugar and coconut milk.

DRIED RICE NOODLES: Also known as rice sticks or rice vermicelli. Soak dried rice noodles in hot water until soft, drain well and use in stir-fries or soups. When deep-fried in their dried state they puff up to a crunchy texture and are used in salads or to top a stir-fry.

BEAN THREAD NOODLES: Made from mung bean starch, bean thread noodles are also known as cellophane noodles. Soak in hot water before use, drain and use in stir-fries, soups or salads.

WHEAT NOODLES: Available in various widths and either plain or enriched with egg, wheat noodles need to be boiled and drained well before inclusion in a dish.

Supermarkets stock a large range of instant noodles or quick cooking noodles. Some include a flavour sachet. They can be added to a quick stir-fry after cooking as directed on the pack.

FRESH ASIAN INGREDIENTS

Fresh flavouring ingredients are important in Asian cooking.

GARLIC: For a mild flavour, fry slices of garlic in the oil then remove before the addition of other ingredients. A more defined flavour is achieved if garlic is finely chopped and included with the other ingredients. Use fresh garlic. Garlic cloves are best stored in a jar in the refrigerator.

GINGER: Ginger is an essential flavouring ingredient. Cut a 1–2 cm (½–¾ in) piece from the ginger root. Peel thinly and slice very finely or grate. Any remaining ginger root may be wrapped in damp paper, placed in a plastic bag and stored in the refrigerator crisper for 2–3 weeks.

LEMONGRASS: This imparts a characteristic sour flavour to Asian dishes. Trim away the outer blades and cut the white bulbous part into thin slices or chop finely. Lemongrass will keep in the refrigerator crisper for up to 2 months.

CHILLIES: Small, red, hot chillies must be handled with care. If an intense hot flavour is needed, chop the chilli with the seeds and vein. If a milder heat is desired, split the chilli and remove the seeds and thick vein. The hot part of the chilli is concentrated in the seeds and vein, and will remain on your fingers. If, after handling chillies, you touch your tongue, lips or eyes, severe irritation will result. Wash your hands immediately after handling chillies or wear rubber gloves.

COCONUT MILK AND CREAM: Is made from fresh, grated coconut 'meat'. Canned coconut milk is available as either thin or thick. Thin coconut milk is used for long simmering with other ingredients. Thick coconut milk or cream is added at the end of the recipe to give flavour and a smooth consistency. Store leftover coconut milk or cream in a sealed container in the refrigerator for up to 1 week. It may also be frozen for longer storage, but loses some of its smooth texture.

FRESH NOODLES: A wide variety may be found in the refrigerator cabinets at supermarkets as well as in Asian food stores. Varieties include Hokkien noodles

and the thinner Singapore noodles, both made from wheat flour. Rice noodles include the Japanese udon and the flat pad thai, which are gluten free.

MEAT: Many Asian recipes call for thinly sliced meat, particularly for a stir-fry. Always cut the meat across the grain for a tender result. Purchase the meat in a thick piece or 'nut' (not a slice), to be able to cut across the grain. For thinly sliced meat, freeze the meat for 2 hours to keep it firm under the blade of the knife. Trays of stir-fry strips or small cubed meats are available in butcher shops and supermarkets.

WRAPPERS: These are squares of noodle dough used to wrap food in to make spring rolls and wontons. Both rice and wheat-based wrappers are available. They can be found in the refrigerator cabinets at supermarkets and Asian food stores.

Japanese prawn and vegetable tempura

INGREDIENTS

1 courgette (zucchini)
salt
4 green prawns (shrimps)
1 red capsicum (pepper)
1 large egg
½ cup (125 ml, 4 fl oz) ice-cold water
150 g (5 oz) plain flour
peanut oil for deep-frying
lime wedges to serve
soy sauce to serve
serves 4

PREPARATION TIME
25 minutes, plus
20 minutes standing

COOKING TIME
10 minutes

1 Cut the courgette (zucchini) in half across the centre, trim the end and cut each half lengthways into 4. Sprinkle with salt and set aside for 20 minutes. Shell the prawns (shrimps), leaving tails attached. Devein, using a sharp knife. Rinse and refrigerate. Deseed the capsicum (pepper) and cut into 8 strips.

2 Break the egg into a mixing bowl. Mix in the ice-cold water and fold in the flour to make a lumpy batter.

3 Heat 5 cm (2 in) of oil in a wok or frying pan. Coat the courgette (zucchini) slices in batter and deep-fry for 3 minutes or until golden, turning halfway through. Drain on kitchen towels and keep warm. Repeat with capsicum (pepper) strips. Coat prawns (shrimps) and cook for 1 minute. Serve immediately with lime wedges and soy sauce.

NUTRITIONAL VALUE PER SERVE	FAT 1.4 G	CARBOHYDRATE 19 G	PROTEIN 7.2 G

Spring rolls

INGREDIENTS

20 g (²/₃ oz) vermicelli
3 tablespoons vegetable oil
3 cloves garlic, finely chopped
310 g (10 oz) minced chicken
¹/₄ cabbage, cut into fine strips
1 carrot, cut into thin strips
2 spring onions (green onions),
 finely chopped
¹/₂ teaspoon salt
1 teaspoon sugar
¹/₂ teaspoon white pepper
1 tablespoon oyster sauce
20–25 rice paper wrappers
1 egg, beaten
extra oil for deep frying
lettuce and mint leaves to serve
makes 20

1 Soak vermicelli in hot water for 5 minutes until soft. Drain, cut into 5 cm (2 in) lengths and set aside.

2 Heat oil in a wok or frying pan, add garlic and chicken and cook for 8 minutes, stirring constantly until crumbly. Add cabbage, carrot, spring onions (green onions) and vermicelli. Cook on high for about 3 minutes until vegetables soften.

3 Turn off heat. Add salt, sugar, pepper and oyster sauce, stir to mix well and allow to cool. Brush each side of the rice wrappers with water. Place 1 tablespoon of mixture onto each wrapper, turn sides in first, roll and seal each with beaten egg. Refrigerate until needed.

4 Heat extra oil in wok or frying pan. Deep-fry a few rolls at a time until golden. Drain on absorbent paper. Serve on lettuce leaves garnished with mint. Serve with your favourite sweet chilli or plum sauce.

PREPARATION TIME
15 minutes

COOKING TIME
15 minutes

NUTRITIONAL VALUE PER SERVE	FAT 9.2 G	CARBOHYDRATE 5 G	PROTEIN 9.8 G

Steamed stuffed cucumbers

INGREDIENTS

500 g (1 lb) cucumbers
cornflour for dusting
375g (12 oz) can water chestnuts,
    drained and finely chopped
2¹/₂ tablespoons glutinous rice
    flour
sesame oil
¹/₂ teaspoon salt
¹/₂ teaspoon sugar
1 small carrot, peeled and
    finely diced
4 black dried mushrooms,
    soaked, drained and finely
    chopped
³/₄ cup (185 ml, 6 fl oz) water
1¹/₂ teaspoons cornflour
serves 4–6

1 Thinly peel cucumbers and cut into 1 cm (¹/₂ in) thick slices. Scoop out seeds with a teaspoon, leaving a base layer. Place cucumber shells in boiling water for 1 minute. Rinse in cold water, drain and dust inside with a little cornflour.

2 In a bowl, place finely diced water chestnuts, glutinous rice flour, sesame oil and half the salt and sugar. Add carrot and mushrooms and mix well. Pile high into the cucumber circles. Place circles on a plate and set on a steaming rack over hot water in a wok. Cover and steam for 15–20 minutes.

3 Place a drop of sesame oil, the remaining salt and sugar and the water into a small saucepan and bring to the boil. Blend the cornflour with a little water, add to the saucepan and stir until liquid boils and thickens. Cool until only warm. Spoon over each steamed cucumber ring to glaze. Allow to cool. Serve at room temperature.

PREPARATION TIME
15 minutes

COOKING TIME
20 minutes

NUTRITIONAL VALUE PER SERVE	FAT 1.7 G	CARBOHYDRATE 7 G	PROTEIN 0.8 G

Balinese chicken satay

INGREDIENTS

1 stalk lemongrass
1 onion, chopped
1 clove garlic, chopped
2 teaspoons ground coriander (cilantro)
1 teaspoon turmeric
juice of ½ lemon
1 teaspoon salt
3 chicken breast fillets, cut into
  1 cm (½ in) cubes
½ cucumber, pared into ribbons
  with a vegetable peeler, to serve

satay sauce
1 small onion, chopped
1 clove garlic, chopped
1 tablespoon peanut oil
1 teaspoon chilli powder
155 ml (5 fl oz) can coconut milk
75 g (2½ oz) roasted salted peanuts,
  finely ground
1 tablespoon soft dark brown sugar
1 tablespoon fresh lemon juice
serves 4

1 Peel the outer layer from the lemongrass and chop the lower white bulbous part, discarding the fibrous top. Process to a paste with the onion, garlic, coriander (cilantro), turmeric, lemon juice and 1 teaspoon of salt in a food processor.

2 Place the chicken in a non-metallic bowl and coat with the paste. Cover and marinate in the refrigerator for 2 hours, or overnight. If using wooden skewers, soak them in water for 10 minutes.

3 To make the satay sauce, process the onion and garlic to a paste in a food processor. Heat the oil in a heavy-based saucepan and fry the paste for 5 minutes, stirring. Mix in the chilli powder, then the remaining sauce ingredients. Bring to the boil, stirring, then simmer for 10 minutes.

4 Preheat the grill to high. Thread the chicken onto 8 skewers. Grill for 10 minutes, turning once, until cooked. Serve with the cucumber ribbons and satay sauce.

PREPARATION TIME
**30 minutes, plus
2 hours marinating**

COOKING TIME
25 minutes

NUTRITIONAL VALUE PER SERVE	FAT 12.9 G	CARBOHYDRATE 4 G	PROTEIN 8.9 G

Vegetable saffron samosas

INGREDIENTS

vegetable saffron filling
1 tablespoon peanut oil
1 teaspoon sesame oil
1 onion, finely chopped
1 tablespoon finely grated
  fresh ginger
1 teaspoon ground cumin
1 potato, peeled and finely chopped
1 carrot, finely chopped
1/4 teaspoon saffron threads, soaked
  in 1 tablespoon hot water
1 red capsicum (pepper),
  finely chopped
60 g (2 oz) frozen peas
pastry
315 g (10 oz) flour
1 tablespoon baking powder
1 tablespoon caster sugar
4 tablespoons butter
1 cup (250 ml, 8 fl oz) warm water
sun-dried capsicum dipping sauce
125 g (4 oz) sun-dried capsicums
  (peppers), chopped
1 cup (250 ml, 8 fl oz) mayonnaise
1 tablespoon white-wine vinegar
makes 20

PREPARATION TIME
30 minutes, plus
10 minutes resting

COOKING TIME
30 minutes

1 To make filling, heat peanut and sesame oils together in a wok over medium heat, add onion, ginger and cumin and stir-fry for 3 minutes or until onion is golden. In a bowl, combine potato, carrot and saffron. Add to wok and stir-fry for 10 minutes until potato is tender. Add red capsicum (pepper) and peas and stir-fry for another 5 minutes. Remove mixture from wok and set aside to cool.

2 To make pastry, place flour, baking powder, sugar and butter in a food processor and process until mixture resembles fine breadcrumbs. With machine running, gradually add water and process until mixture forms a soft dough. Turn dough onto a lightly floured surface and knead until smooth and glossy. Cover and rest for 10 minutes.

3 Divide dough into 20 equal pieces and shape into balls. Roll out each dough ball to form a 10 cm (4 in) circle. Place a tablespoon of filling on one half, leaving a 1 1/2 cm (1/2 in) border. Brush edges lightly with water, fold pastry over filling and press edges together to seal.

4 Half fill a clean wok with hot water and bring to the boil. Place samosas in a bamboo steamer lined with non-stick baking paper. Pierce holes in the paper to allow steam through. Cover steamer, place on a wire rack in wok and steam for 10 minutes or until pastry is cooked.

5 To make sauce, place sun-dried capsicums (peppers), mayonnaise and vinegar in a food processor or blender and process until smooth.

NUTRITIONAL VALUE PER SERVE	FAT 10.6 G	CARBOHYDRATE 25 G	PROTEIN 4.1 G

Creamy chicken korma

INGREDIENTS

3 tablespoons vegetable oil
1 onion, chopped
2 cloves garlic, crushed
3 tablespoons plain flour
2 tablespoons mild korma
  curry powder
750 g (1½ lb) chicken breast fillets,
  cut into 2.5 cm (1 in) cubes
350 ml (11½ fl oz) chicken stock
25 g (1 oz) raisins
1 tablespoon chopped
  fresh coriander (cilantro)
1 teaspoon garam masala
juice of ½ lemon
4 tablespoons sour cream
fried onion rings for garnish
  (optional)
serves 4

PREPARATION TIME
15 minutes

COOKING TIME
30 minutes

1 Heat the oil in a large heavy-based saucepan, add the onion and garlic and cook gently
   for 5 minutes or until softened.

2 Into a bowl, place the flour and curry powder and mix together. Toss the chicken in the
   seasoned flour, coating well. Reserve the remaining flour. Add the chicken to the onion
   and garlic, then cook, stirring, for 3–4 minutes until lightly browned. Stir in the seasoned
   flour and cook for 1 minute.

3 Add the stock and raisins and bring to the boil, stirring. Cover and simmer for 15 minutes.
   Add the coriander (cilantro) and garam masala and cook for a further 5 minutes. Remove
   the pan from the heat and stir in the lemon juice and sour cream. Return to a low heat
   and warm through, taking care not to let the mixture boil. Serve with rice, garnished
   with fried onion rings, if desired.

NUTRITIONAL VALUE PER SERVE	FAT 7.8 G	CARBOHYDRATE 4.1 G	PROTEIN 12 G

Chicken stir-fry with lemon and mango

INGREDIENTS

1 ripe mango
2 tablespoons sunflower oil
2 cloves garlic, crushed
2.5 cm (1 in) piece fresh root ginger,
  finely chopped
4 chicken breast fillets,
  cut into strips
150 g (5 oz) mangetout (snow peas),
  halved lengthways
2 celery sticks, thinly sliced
1 yellow capsicum (pepper), deseeded
  and cut into matchsticks
4 spring onions (green onions),
  thinly sliced
sea salt and freshly ground
  black pepper
juice of ½ lemon
2 teaspoons white wine
  or apple juice
1 tablespoon balsamic vinegar
1 tablespoon clear honey
2 tablespoons chopped
  fresh coriander (cilantro)

serves 4

1 Slice the two fatter 'cheeks' of the mango from either side of the stone. Cut a criss-cross pattern across the flesh of each piece to divide into small cubes, then push the skin inwards and slice off the cubes. Set aside.

2 Heat the oil in a wok or large frying pan until hot. Add garlic, ginger and chicken and stir-fry for 3 minutes. Add mangetout (snow peas), celery and capsicum (pepper) and stir-fry for 3–4 minutes. Add the spring onions (green onions), mangos and seasoning, and then stir-fry for a further 2 minutes.

3 In a small bowl, combine the lemon juice, white wine or apple juice, balsamic vinegar and honey. Add to the wok and continue to cook for a further 2 minutes. Add the coriander (cilantro) and serve.

PREPARATION TIME
25 minutes

COOKING TIME
10 minutes

NUTRITIONAL VALUE PER SERVE	FAT **4.4** G	CARBOHYDRATE **3.1** G	PROTEIN **14.1** G

Beef with black bean sauce

INGREDIENTS

450 g (14 oz) sirloin or rump steak,
  cut into thin strips
1 clove garlic, crushed
1 small red chilli, deseeded and
  finely chopped (optional)
1 tablespoon dark soy sauce
black pepper
2 teaspoons cornflour
1 tablespoon white-wine vinegar
2 tablespoons vegetable oil
1 red capsicum (pepper),
  deseeded and cut into strips
1 yellow capsicum (pepper), deseeded
  and cut into strips
1 large courgette (zucchini),
  cut into matchsticks
150 g (5 oz) mangetout (snow peas),
  sliced
3 tablespoons black bean
  stir-fry sauce
4 spring onions (green onions),
  diagonally sliced

serves 4

1 In a bowl, combine steak strips, garlic, chilli
(if using), soy sauce and seasoning. In another
bowl, mix the cornflour with 1 tablespoon of
water until smooth, then stir in vinegar.

2 Heat the oil in a wok or large frying pan until
very hot. Add the meat and its marinade and
stir-fry for 4 minutes, tossing continuously,
until seared on all sides.

3 Add capsicum (pepper) and stir-fry for 2
minutes. Stir in courgette (zucchini) and
mangetout (snow peas) and cook for 3 minutes.
Reduce the heat and add the cornflour
mixture and black bean sauce. Stir to mix
thoroughly and cook for 2 minutes or until
the meat and vegetables are cooked through.
Scatter with spring onions (green onions)
just before serving. Serve with egg noodles if
desired.

PREPARATION TIME
15 minutes

COOKING TIME
15 minutes

NUTRITIONAL VALUE PER SERVE	FAT 5.1 G	CARBOHYDRATE 3.5 G	PROTEIN 9.4 G

Thai green duck curry with bamboo shoots

INGREDIENTS

2 tablespoons vegetable oil
3 tablespoons Thai green curry paste
4 boneless duck breasts, skinned and
    cut into 2.5 cm (1 in) cubes
400 ml (13 fl oz) can coconut milk
225 g (7¹/₂ oz) can sliced bamboo
    shoots, drained
2 tablespoons Thai fish sauce
1 teaspoon soft dark brown sugar
salt to taste
2 tablespoons chopped fresh basil
4 tablespoons chopped
    fresh coriander (cilantro)
extra basil leaves to garnish
serves 4

PREPARATION TIME
10 minutes

COOKING TIME
45 minutes

1 Heat the oil in a large, heavy-based saucepan. Add curry paste
   and fry, stirring frequently, for 3 minutes or until the aromas
   are released. Add duck, turn to coat thoroughly, and fry for
   4–5 minutes, stirring from time to time.

2 Stir in coconut milk, bamboo shoots, fish sauce, sugar and salt
   to taste. Bring to the boil, stirring often, then reduce the heat.
   Simmer, uncovered, for 30–35 minutes until the duck is tender,
   stirring occasionally. Just before serving, stir in the chopped basil
   and coriander (cilantro), and garnish with basil leaves.

NUTRITIONAL VALUE PER SERVE   FAT **18.3** G   CARBOHYDRATE 2 G   PROTEIN **10.4** G

Fried noodles with chicken stir-fry

INGREDIENTS

200 g (7 oz) wheat noodles
250 g (8 oz) chicken breast fillets
  cut into 5 cm (2 in) wide strips
1/2 teaspoon salt
1/2 teaspoon five-spice powder
2 tablespoons oil
1 clove garlic, halved
4 mushrooms, sliced
4 spring onions (green onions)
1 red capsicum (pepper),
  deseeded and cut into strips
2 baby bok choy (pak choi),
  leaves separated
425 g (14 oz) can baby corn, drained
1 tablespoon dry sherry
2 teaspoons cornflour
1 tablespoon oyster sauce
serves 4

1 Soak wheat noodles in hot water for 5 minutes, drain well. Sprinkle chicken strips with salt and five-spice powder.

2 Heat the wok, add 2 teaspoons of oil. Place in the noodles and stir-fry until hot and coloured a little. Remove and keep hot.

3 Add 2 teaspoons of oil to the wok, add garlic and fry for 1 minute, then remove. Add chicken and stir-fry for 2 minutes. Remove and keep hot.

4 Add more oil to the wok if needed. Add mushrooms, spring onions (green onions) and capsicums (peppers), and stir-fry for 1 minute. Toss in bok choy and baby corn.

5 In a small bowl, combine sherry and cornflour until smooth, then add oyster sauce. Return chicken to the wok and toss, stir in blended sauce and toss well to distribute. Stir-fry for 1–2 minutes to thicken and reheat. Pile over hot noodles and serve immediately.

PREPARATION TIME
15 minutes

COOKING TIME
10 minutes

| NUTRITIONAL VALUE PER SERVE | FAT **3.9** G | CARBOHYDRATE **15** G | PROTEIN **6.5** G |

Chicken laksa

INGREDIENTS

⅓ cup (90 ml, 3 fl oz) vegetable oil
4 small fresh red chillies,
  finely chopped
1 stalk fresh lemongrass,
  finely chopped or ½ teaspoon
  dried lemongrass, soaked in
  hot water until soft
3 cloves garlic, crushed
2 tablespoons finely grated
  fresh ginger
1 teaspoon ground cumin
1 teaspoon ground turmeric
6 candlenuts or unsalted
  macadamia nuts
¼ teaspoon shrimp paste
1 litre (1⅔ pints) coconut milk
4 boneless chicken breast fillets,
  cut into 2 cm (1 in) cubes
2 tablespoons chopped fresh
  coriander (cilantro)
375 g (12 oz) rice noodles, cooked
125 g (4 oz) bean sprouts
125 g (4 oz) fried tofu, sliced
serves 4

1 Into a food processor, place 2 tablespoons oil, chillies, lemongrass, garlic, ginger, cumin, turmeric, candlenuts or macadamia nuts and shrimp paste, and process to make a smooth paste.

2 In a large saucepan, heat the remaining oil over a medium heat, add paste and cook, stirring, for 2 minutes or until fragrant. Stir in coconut milk and simmer, stirring occasionally, for 15 minutes or until mixture thickens slightly.

3 Add chicken and coriander (cilantro) and simmer, stirring occasionally, for 15 minutes longer or until chicken is tender. To serve, divide rice noodles between serving bowls, top with bean sprouts and tofu, pour over coconut milk mixture and serve immediately.

PREPARATION TIME
20 minutes

COOKING TIME
30 minutes

NUTRITIONAL VALUE PER SERVE	FAT 14.9 G	CARBOHYDRATE 4 G	PROTEIN 10.5 G

South-East Asian pan-fried prawns

INGREDIENTS

500 g (1 lb) green prawns (shrimps)
3 small red chillies, deseeded and
  chopped
2 cloves garlic, chopped
2.5 cm (1 in) piece fresh root ginger,
  chopped
1 spring onion (green onion),
  chopped
2 tablespoons peanut oil
1 onion, chopped
2 tomatoes, quartered
1 teaspoon sugar
salt
serves 4

PREPARATION TIME
25 minutes

COOKING TIME
8 minutes

1 Shell the prawns (shrimps), leaving the tails attached. Cut a slit along
   the back of each prawn (shrimp) with a sharp knife and remove the
   thin black vein. Rinse well and refrigerate. In a food processor, blend
   the chillies, garlic, ginger and spring onion (green onion) to a paste.

2 Heat a wok over a high heat, add oil and onion and fry for 2 minutes
   to soften slightly. Add paste and stir-fry for 1 minute to release the
   flavours. Add prawns (shrimps) and tomatoes, mixing thoroughly,
   then sprinkle over sugar and salt to taste. Stir-fry for 3–5 minutes,
   until prawns (shrimps) turn pink and are cooked through.

NUTRITIONAL VALUE PER SERVE	FAT 4.1 G	CARBOHYDRATE 1.9 G	PROTEIN 10.2 G

Baked cod with ginger and spring onions

INGREDIENTS

oil for greasing
500 g (1 lb) piece cod fillet
1 tablespoon light soy sauce
1 tablespoon rice wine or
  medium-dry sherry
1 teaspoon sesame oil
salt
3 spring onions (green onions),
  shredded and cut into 2.5 cm
  (1 in) pieces, white and green parts
  separated
2.5 cm (1 in) piece fresh root ginger,
  finely chopped
serves 4

PREPARATION TIME
10 minutes

COOKING TIME
20–25 minutes

1 Preheat the oven to 190°C (375°F, gas mark 5). Line a shallow
  baking tray with a piece of lightly greased foil to come past the
  sides of the baking tray. Place the cod on the tray, skin-side down.
  Pour over the soy sauce, rice wine or sherry, oil and salt to taste,
  then sprinkle over the white spring onion (green onion)
  and ginger.

2 Loosely wrap the foil over the fish, folding the edges together to
  seal. Bake for 20–25 minutes, until cooked through and tender.
  Unwrap the parcel, transfer the fish to a serving plate and
  sprinkle with green parts of spring onion (green onions).

NUTRITIONAL VALUE PER SERVE   FAT **1.4** G   CARBOHYDRATE **0.6** G   PROTEIN **15.1** G

Seafood with oyster mushrooms

INGREDIENTS

125 g (4 oz) small calamari (squid) hoods

8 baby octopus

8 medium-sized green prawns (shrimps), shelled and deveined

155 g (5 oz) fresh scallops

2 teaspoons vegetable oil

250 g (8 oz) oyster mushrooms

6 spring onions (green onions), chopped

freshly ground black pepper

marinade

3 tablespoons chopped fresh coriander (cilantro)

2 cloves garlic, crushed

4 tablespoons worcestershire sauce

$1/3$ cup (90 ml, 3 fl oz) soy sauce

2 tablespoons sweet chilli sauce

serves 4–6

1 Cut down the length of the squid's hood and open out. Score the inside surface into a diamond pattern, taking care not to cut right through the flesh. Clean the baby octopus by cutting off the head below the eyes and discarding. Push out and remove the beak located in the centre of the tentacles. Wash well.

2 In a bowl, combine all marinade ingredients and add calamari (squid), octopus, prawns (shrimps) and scallops. Toss to coat with marinade, cover and refrigerate for 2–3 hours.

3 Drain seafood and reserve the marinade. Heat a wok until very hot, then add oil, swirling to coat base and sides. Add calamari (squid) and octopus and stir-fry for 2 minutes, then add prawns (shrimps) and scallops. Stir-fry for 1 minute.

4 Add mushrooms, spring onions (green onions) and 3 tablespoons reserved marinade and stir-fry for 2 minutes more. Season to taste with black pepper. Transfer to a serving dish and serve immediately.

PREPARATION TIME
15 minutes, plus
2–3 hours marinating

COOKING TIME
5 minutes

NUTRITIONAL VALUE PER SERVE	FAT 1.5 G	CARBOHYDRATE 3.2 G	PROTEIN 10.7 G

Fragrant salmon stir-fry

INGREDIENTS

250 g (8 oz) skinless salmon fillets
1¹/₂ tablespoons peanut or
  sunflower oil
1 tablespoon chilled butter, cubed
marinade
1 stalk lemongrass
1 tablespoon soy sauce
¹/₂ cup (125 ml, 4 fl oz) orange juice
1 tablespoon chopped fresh dill
1 tablespoon chopped fresh basil
1 teaspoon grated fresh root ginger
1 clove garlic, crushed
salt and black pepper
serves 2

PREPARATION TIME
**10 minutes, 2 hours
marinating**

COOKING TIME
10 minutes

1 Peel the outer layer from the lemongrass stalk, then finely chop the lower white bulbous
   part. In a bowl, combine lemongrass, soy sauce, orange juice, ¹/₂ tablespoon dill,
   ¹/₂ tablespoon basil, ginger, garlic and seasoning. Cut the salmon fillet into strips 2.5 cm
   (1 in) wide and 7.5 cm (3 in) long. Arrange strips in a shallow non-metallic dish and pour
   the marinade over the top, turning strips to coat. Cover and refrigerate for 2 hours.

2 Remove salmon from dish and set aside the marinade. Pat salmon dry. Heat the oil in a
   large, heavy-based frying pan over a medium to high heat, add salmon and cook for
   2 minutes on each side.

3 Arrange salmon on serving plates. Pour reserved marinade into the frying pan, bring to
   the boil and simmer for 2 minutes. Whisk in butter, a cube at a time. Spoon sauce over
   the salmon and sprinkle remaining dill and basil.

NUTRITIONAL VALUE PER SERVE	FAT **12.6** G	CARBOHYDRATE **2.5** G	PROTEIN **11.2** G

Herbed rice noodles
with asparagus and peanuts

INGREDIENTS

3 tablespoons rice vinegar

1 tablespoon sugar

1 small red onion, finely sliced into rings

255 g (8 oz) dried rice noodles

2 bunches of asparagus

a handful fresh mint, chopped

a handful fresh coriander (cilantro), chopped

1 continental cucumber, peeled, seeded and thinly sliced

6 spring onions (green onions), finely sliced

3 roma tomatoes, finely diced

120 g (4 oz) roasted peanuts, lightly crushed

juice of 2 limes

2 teaspoons fish sauce

2 teaspoons olive oil

½ teaspoon chilli flakes

serves 4

1 Whisk the rice vinegar and sugar together and pour over the onion rings. Allow to marinate for 1 hour, tossing frequently. Cook rice noodles in boiling water for 1–2 minutes, then drain immediately and rinse under cold water. Cut into a manageable length with kitchen scissors.

2 Peel the tough skin off the lower third of the asparagus stalk with a potato peeler, then cut into 2 cm (1 in) lengths. Simmer asparagus in salted water for 2 minutes until bright green and crisp-tender. Rinse in cold water to refresh.

3 Toss the noodles with the onion and vinegar mixture while still warm. Add asparagus, mint, coriander (cilantro), cucumber, spring onions (green onions), tomatoes and roasted peanuts and toss thoroughly. In a small bowl, whisk the lime juice, fish sauce, oil and chilli flakes together and drizzle over the noodle salad. Serve at room temperature.

PREPARATION TIME
20 minutes, plus
1 hour marinating

COOKING TIME
4 minutes

NUTRITIONAL VALUE PER SERVE	FAT 3.8 G	CARBOHYDRATE 6 G	PROTEIN 3 G

Vegetable stir-fry with noodles

INGREDIENTS

250 g (8 oz) broad ribbon egg noodles
2 tablespoons sunflower oil
1 clove garlic, sliced
2 carrots, thinly sliced diagonally
150 g (5 oz) green beans, halved
150 g (5 oz) broccoli florets
1 red capsicum (pepper), deseeded and
  cut into thin strips
4 spring onions (green onions), sliced
  thinly and diagonally

sauce

4 tablespoons smooth peanut butter
1 tablespoon tomato purée
1 tablespoon balsamic vinegar
sea salt and freshly ground
  black pepper
fresh coriander (cilantro), chopped
lemon wedges, to serve

serves 4

1 Cook the noodles. In a bowl, combine the peanut butter, tomato purée, balsamic vinegar and seasoning with about 4 tablespoons of cold water. Set aside.

2 Heat a wok or large frying pan until very hot. Add oil, garlic, carrots and green beans and stir-fry for 2 minutes, until lightly coloured. Add broccoli and stir-fry for 2–3 minutes or until softened. Add capsicum (pepper) and spring onions (green onions), then cook for a further 1 minute.

3 Add the sauce, ½ cup (125 ml, 4 fl oz) water and noodles. Combine well and stir-fry for 4–5 minutes or until everything is hot. Garnish with fresh coriander (cilantro) and serve with lemon wedges.

PREPARATION TIME
25 minutes

COOKING TIME
15 minutes

NUTRITIONAL VALUE PER SERVE   FAT **9.1** G   CARBOHYDRATE **15** G   PROTEIN **6.5** G

Baked passionfruit custards

INGREDIENTS

4 large eggs, beaten
4 tablespoons caster sugar
150 ml (5 fl oz) coconut milk
pinch of salt
2 passionfruit
serves 4

1 Preheat the oven to 180°C (350°F, gas mark 4). Whisk together the eggs, sugar, coconut milk and salt until smooth, then pour into 4 ramekins.

2 Halve 1 passionfruit, scoop out the pulp and seeds and divide between the 4 custard-filled ramekins. Place ramekins in a deep roasting tin.

3 Pour boiling water into the roasting tin to three-quarters of the way up the sides of the ramekins. Bake the custards for 40 minutes. Serve warm or cold with the pulp and seeds from the remaining passionfruit spooned over the top.

PREPARATION TIME
10 minutes

COOKING TIME
40 minutes

NUTRITIONAL VALUE PER SERVE   FAT **11.1** G   CARBOHYDRATE **15** G   PROTEIN **6.9** G

Oriental fruit salad

INGREDIENTS

3 stalks lemongrass
60 g (2 oz) caster sugar
1 small rock melon (cantaloupe)
1 mango
425 g (14 oz) can lychees, drained
fresh mint leaves to garnish
serves 4

1 Peel the outer layers from the lemongrass stalks and finely chop the lower white bulbous parts. In a pan, place the lemongrass, sugar and 100 ml ($3^1/_2$ fl oz) water. Simmer, stirring, for 5 minutes or until sugar dissolves, then bring to the boil. Remove from heat and leave to cool for 20 minutes. Refrigerate for 30 minutes.

2 Halve the melon and scrape out the seeds. Cut into wedges, remove skin and cut the flesh into small chunks. Slice off the two fat sides of the mango close to the stone. Cut a criss-cross pattern across the flesh of each piece, then push the skin in to expose the cubes of flesh and cut them off. Place the melon, mango and lychees in serving bowls. Strain the lemongrass syrup and pour over the fruit. Decorate with mint.

PREPARATION TIME
30 minutes, plus
20 minutes cooling
and 30 minutes
chilling

COOKING TIME
5 minutes

NUTRITIONAL VALUE PER SERVE   FAT **0.2** G   CARBOHYDRATE **13** G   PROTEIN **0.7** G

Glossary

Al dente: Italian term to describe pasta and rice that are cooked until tender but still firm to the bite.

Bake blind: to bake pastry cases without their fillings. Line the raw pastry case with greaseproof paper and fill with raw rice or dried beans to prevent collapsed sides and puffed base. Remove paper and fill 5 minutes before completion of cooking time.

Baste: to spoon hot cooking liquid over food at intervals during cooking to moisten and flavour it.

Beat: to make a mixture smooth with rapid and regular motions using a spatula, wire whisk or electric mixer; to make a mixture light and smooth by enclosing air.

Beurre manié: equal quantities of butter and flour mixed together to a smooth paste and stirred bit by bit into a soup, stew or sauce while on the heat to thicken. Stop adding when desired thickness results.

Bind: to add egg or a thick sauce to hold ingredients together when cooked.

Blanch: to plunge some foods into boiling water for less than a minute and immediately plunge into iced water. This is to brighten the colour of some vegetables and to remove skin from tomatoes and nuts.

Blend: to mix 2 or more ingredients thoroughly together; do not confuse with blending in an electric blender.

Boil: to cook in a liquid brought to boiling point and kept there.

Boiling point: when bubbles rise continually and break over the entire surface of the liquid, reaching a temperature of 100°C (212°F). In some cases food is held at this high temperature for a few seconds then heat is turned to low for slower cooking. See *simmer*.

Bouquet garni: a bundle of several herbs tied together with string for easy removal, placed into pots of stock, soups and stews for flavour. A few sprigs of fresh thyme, parsley and bay leaf are used. Can be purchased in sachet form for convenience.

Caramelise: to heat sugar in a heavy-based pan until it liquefies and develops a caramel colour. Vegetables such as blanched carrots and sautéed onions may be sprinkled with sugar and caramelised.

Chill: to place in the refrigerator or stir over ice until cold.

Clarify: to make a liquid clear by removing sediments and impurities. To melt fat and remove any sediment.

Coat: to dust or roll food items in flour to cover the surface before the food is cooked. Also, to coat in flour, egg and breadcrumbs.

Cool: to stand at room temperature until some or all heat is removed, eg cool a little, cool completely.

Cream: to make creamy and fluffy by working the mixture with the back of a wooden spoon; usually refers to creaming butter and sugar or margarine. May also be done with an electric mixer.

Croutons: small cubes of bread, toasted or fried, used as an addition to salads or as a garnish to soups and stews.

Crudités: raw vegetable sticks served with a dipping sauce.

Crumb: to coat foods in flour, egg and breadcrumbs to form a protective coating for foods which are fried. Also adds flavour and texture and enhances appearance.

Cube: to cut into small pieces with six even sides, eg cubes of meat.

Cut in: to combine fat, such as butter or shortening, and flour using 2 knives scissor-fashion or a pastry blender, to make pastry.

Deglaze: to dissolve dried-out cooking juices left on the base and sides of a roasting dish or frying pan. Add a little water, wine or stock, scrape and stir over heat until dissolved. Resulting liquid is used to make a flavoursome gravy or added to a sauce or casserole.

Degrease: to skim fat from the surface of cooking liquids, eg stocks, soups, casseroles.

Dice: to cut into small cubes.

Dredge: to heavily coat with icing sugar, sugar, flour or cornflour.

Dressing: a mixture added to completed dishes to add moisture and flavour, eg salads, cooked vegetables.

Drizzle: to pour in a fine thread-like stream moving over a surface.

Egg wash: beaten egg with milk or water used to brush over pastry, bread dough or biscuits to give a sheen and golden brown colour.

Essence: a strong flavouring liquid, usually made by distillation. Only a few drops are needed to flavour.

Fillet: a piece of prime meat, fish or poultry which is boneless or has all bones removed.

Flake: to separate cooked fish into flakes, removing any bones and skin, using 2 forks.

Flame: to ignite warmed alcohol over food or to pour into a pan with food, ignite, then serve.

Flute: to make decorative indentations around the pastry rim before baking.

Fold in: combining of a light, whisked or creamed mixture with other ingredients. Add a portion of the other ingredients at a time and mix using a gentle circular motion, over and under the mixture so that air will not be lost. Use a metal spoon or spatula.

Glaze: to brush or coat food with a liquid that will give the finished product a glossy appearance, and on baked products, a golden brown colour.

Grease: to rub the surface of a metal or heatproof dish with oil or fat, to prevent the food from sticking.

Herbed butter: softened butter mixed with finely chopped fresh herbs and re-chilled. Used to serve on grilled meats and fish.

Hors d'oeuvre: small savoury foods served as an appetiser, popularly known today as 'finger food'.

Infuse: to steep foods in a liquid until the liquid absorbs their flavour.

Joint: to cut poultry and game into serving pieces by dividing at the joint.

Julienne: to cut some food, eg vegetables and processed meats, into fine strips the length of matchsticks. Used in salads or as a garnish to cooked dishes.

Knead: to work a yeast dough in a pressing, stretching and folding motion with the heel of the hand until smooth and elastic to develop the gluten strands. Non-yeast doughs should be lightly and quickly handled as gluten development is not desired.

Line: to cover the inside of a baking tin with paper for the easy removal of the cooked product from the baking tin.

Macerate: to stand fruit in a syrup, liqueur or spirit to give added flavour.

Marinade: a flavoured liquid, into which food is placed for some time to give it flavour and to tenderise. Marinades include an acid ingredient such as vinegar or wine, oil and seasonings.

Mask: to evenly cover cooked food portions with a sauce, mayonnaise or savoury jelly.

Pan-fry: to fry foods in a small amount of fat or oil, sufficient to coat the base of the pan.

Parboil: to boil until partially cooked. The food is then finished by some other method.

Pare: to peel the skin from vegetables and fruit. 'Peel' is the popular term but 'pare' is the name given to the knife used; paring knife.

Pit: to remove stones or seeds from olives, cherries, dates.

Pith: the white lining between the rind and flesh of oranges, grapefruit and lemons.

Pitted: the olives, cherries, dates etc. with the stone removed, eg purchase pitted dates.

Poach: to simmer gently in enough hot liquid to almost cover the food so its shape will be retained.

Pound: to flatten meats with a meat mallet; to reduce to a paste or small particles with a mortar and pestle.

Simmer: to cook in liquid just below boiling point at about 96°C (205°F) with small bubbles rising gently to the surface.

Skim: to remove fat or froth from the surface of simmering food.

Stock: the liquid produced when meat, poultry, fish or vegetables have been simmered in water to extract the flavour. Used as a base for soups, sauces, casseroles etc. Convenience stock products are available.

Sweat: to cook sliced onions or vegetables in a small amount of butter in a covered pan over low heat, to soften them and release flavour without colouring.

Conversions

Measurements differ from country to country, so it's important to understand what the differences are. This Measurements Guide gives you simple 'at-a-glance' information for using the recipes in this book, wherever you may be.

Cooking is not an exact science – minor variations in measurements won't make a difference to your cooking.

EQUIPMENT

There is a difference in the size of measuring cups used internationally, but the difference is minimal (only 2–3 teaspoons). We use the Australian standard metric measurements in our recipes:

1 teaspoon.....5 ml   1 tablespoon.....20 ml
$^1/_2$ cup.....125 ml   1 cup.....250 ml
4 cups.....1 litre

Measuring cups come in sets of one cup (250 ml), $^1/_2$ cup (125 ml), $^1/_3$ cup (80 ml) and $^1/_4$ cup (60 ml). Use these for measuring liquids and certain dry ingredients.

Measuring spoons come in a set of four and should be used for measuring dry and liquid ingredients.

When using cup or spoon measures, always make them level (unless the recipe indicates otherwise).

DRY VERSUS WET INGREDIENTS

While this system of measures is consistent for liquids, it's more difficult to quantify dry ingredients. For instance, one level cup equals: 200 g of brown sugar; 210 g of caster sugar; and 110 g of icing sugar.

When measuring dry ingredients such as flour, don't push the flour down or shake it into the cup. It is best just to spoon the flour in until it reaches the desired amount. When measuring liquids, use a clear vessel indicating metric levels.

Always use medium eggs (55–60 g) when eggs are required in a recipe.

OVEN

Your oven should always be at the right temperature before placing the food in it to be cooked. Note that if your oven doesn't have a fan you may need to cook food for a little longer.

MICROWAVE

It is difficult to give an exact cooking time for microwave cooking. It is best to watch what you are cooking closely to monitor its progress.

STANDING TIME

Many foods continue to cook when you take them out of the oven or microwave. If a recipe states that the food needs to 'stand' after cooking, be sure not to overcook the dish.

CAN SIZES

The can sizes available in your supermarket or grocery store may not be the same as specified in the recipe. Don't worry if there is a small variation in size – it's unlikely to make a difference to the end result.

dry		liquids	
metric (grams)	imperial (ounces)	metric (millilitres)	imperial (fluid ounces)
		30 ml	1 fl oz
30 g	1 oz	60 ml	2 fl oz
60 g	2 oz	90 ml	3 fl oz
90 g	3 oz	100 ml	3 1/2 fl oz
100 g	3 1/2 oz	125 ml	4 fl oz
125 g	4 oz	150 ml	5 fl oz
150 g	5 oz	190 ml	6 fl oz
185 g	6 oz	250 ml	8 fl oz
200 g	7 oz	300 ml	10 fl oz
250 g	8 oz	500 ml	16 fl oz
280 g	9 oz	600 ml	20 fl oz (1 pint)*
315 g	10 oz	1000 ml (1 litre)	32 fl oz
330 g	11 oz		
370 g	12 oz		
400 g	13 oz		
440 g	14 oz		
470 g	15 oz		
500 g	16 oz (1 lb)		
750 g	24 oz (1 1/2 lb)		
1000 g (1 kg)	32 oz (2 lb)	*Note: an American pint is 16 fl oz.	

cooking temperatures	°C (celsius)	°F (fahrenheit)	gas mark
very slow	120	250	1/2
slow	150	300	2
moderately slow	160	315	2–3
moderate	180	350	4
moderately hot	190	375	5
	200	400	6
hot	220	425	7
very hot	230	450	8
	240	475	9
	250	500	10

Index

A

asparagus 38

B

baked cod with ginger
    and spring onions 32–33
baked passionfruit custards 40
Balinese chicken satay 14–15
bamboo shoots 24-25
beef with black bean sauce 22–23

C

chicken
    Balinese chicken satay 14–15
    chicken laksa 28–29
    chicken stir-fry with
        lemon and mango 20–21
    creamy chicken korma 18–19
    fried noodles with
        chicken stir-fry 26–27
conversions 44–45
creamy chicken korma 18–19
cucumber
    steamed stuffed cucumbers 13
curry
    Thai green duck curry with
        bamboo shoots 24–25
custard 40

D

desserts 40–41
duck
    Thai green duck curry with
        bamboo shoots 24–25

F

fish
    baked cod with ginger and
        spring onions 32–33
    fragrant salmon stir-fry 36–37
flavouring agents 5–6
fragrant salmon stir-fry 36–37
fried noodles with
    chicken stir-fry 26–27
fruit salad 41

G

ginger
    baked cod with ginger and
        spring onions 32–33
glossary 42–43

H

herbed rice noodles with
    asparagus and peanuts 38

I

introduction 4–9

J

Japanese prawn and vegetable
    tempura 10–11

K

korma 18–19

L

laksa 28–29
lemon 20–21

M

mango
    chicken stir-fry with
        lemon and mango 20–21
measurements 44–45
meat 18–19
mushrooms 34–35

N

noodles 6–8
    fried noodles with chicken
        stir-fry 26–27
    herbed rice noodles with
        asparagus and peanuts 38
    vegetable stir-fry with
        noodles 39

O

oriental fruit salad 41
oyster mushrooms 34–35

P

pantry 4
passionfruit custards 40
peanut
    herbed rice noodles with
        asparagus and peanuts 38
prawn
    Japanese prawn and
        vegetable tempura 10–11
South-East Asian pan-fried
    prawns 30–31

R

rice 6–8
rice noodles 38
rolls
    spring 12

S

saffron 16–17
salads
    oriental fruit salad 41
salmon
    fragrant salmon stir-fry 36–37
samosas 16–17
satay 14–15
sauces 4–5
    black bean sauce 22–23
seafood 30–37
    baked cod with ginger and
        spring onions 32–33
    fragrant salmon stir-fry 36–37
    Japanese prawn and
    vegetable tempura 10–11
    seafood with oyster
        mushrooms 34–35
South-East Asian pan-fried
    prawns 30–31
spices 5–6
spring onions 32–33
spring rolls 12
steamed stuffed cucumbers 13
stir-fry
    chicken with lemon
        and mango 20–21
    fragrant salmon 36–37
    fried noodles with
        chicken 26–27
    vegetable with noodles 39

T

Thai green duck curry with
    bamboo shoots 24–25

V

vegetable saffron samosas 16–17
vegetable stir-fry with noodles 39
vegetarian 38–39

W

weights 44–45

Essential COOKING SERIES

COMPREHENSIVE, STEP-BY-STEP COOKING

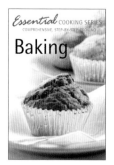

Essential COOKING SERIES
COMPREHENSIVE, STEP-BY-STEP COOKING
Baking

Essential COOKING SERIES
COMPREHENSIVE, STEP-BY-STEP COOKING
Chicken Meals

Essential COOKING SERIES
COMPREHENSIVE, STEP-BY-STEP COOKING
Salads & Greens

Essential COOKING SERIES
COMPREHENSIVE, STEP-BY-STEP COOKING
Soups & Hors D'Oeuvres

Essential COOKING SERIES
COMPREHENSIVE, STEP-BY-STEP COOKING
Meat Dishes

Essential COOKING SERIES
COMPREHENSIVE, STEP-BY-STEP COOKING
Finger Food

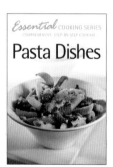

Essential COOKING SERIES
COMPREHENSIVE, STEP-BY-STEP COOKING
Pasta Dishes

Essential COOKING SERIES
COMPREHENSIVE, STEP-BY-STEP COOKING
Grilling & Barbecuing

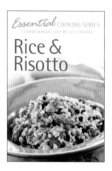

Essential COOKING SERIES
COMPREHENSIVE, STEP-BY-STEP COOKING
Rice & Risotto

Essential COOKING SERIES
COMPREHENSIVE, STEP-BY-STEP COOKING
Vegetarian Dishes

Essential COOKING SERIES
COMPREHENSIVE, STEP-BY-STEP COOKING
Asian Dishes

Essential COOKING SERIES
COMPREHENSIVE, STEP-BY-STEP COOKING
Stir-Fry